2022
Astrology

Scorpio
October 24 to November 22

SCORPIO

October 24 – November 22

Publishing Director: Isabelle Dion
Author: Chantale Montpetit
Editors: Erika Szucs, Diandra D'Alessio, Clarissa Sorgiovanni
Proofreaders: Diandra D'Alessio, Clarissa Sorgiovanni
Cover Designers: Doran Woo, Stéphane Gauthier
Graphic Designer: Dominique Roy

Funded by the Government of Canada | Canadä

PAPP International Inc.
3700 Griffith St., Suite 395,
Montreal (Quebec), Canada H4T 2B3

Table of Contents

2022
Forecasts

January

As you tend to talk too much, you'll have to be careful at the beginning of the year. Any secrets that a loved one tells you should be kept to yourself. You shouldn't share them with anyone else. Know how to hold your tongue because this could get you into trouble.

HEALTH
You may experience low blood pressure, and this can be very concerning. Don't hesitate to consult a doctor to receive the appropriate advice. Your mental health is not at its best. Too many emotional burdens could overwhelm you and throw off your balance. Take care of yourself; you'll need to.

WORK AND MONEY
You may experience bullying at work, and it will affect you. It will be imperative to report it so that the person concerned can be held accountable. You will be less disciplined in your work than you usually are, and it will be pointed out to you. You'll find it difficult to concentrate with all these disruptions affecting you.

LOVE • SINGLES
Even though an interesting person is eyeing you, your reaction will be mixed. You'll be physically attracted to them, but you won't be emotionally engaged. You'll realize that a future together isn't possible despite all their good intentions.

LOVE • COUPLES
Life as a couple is not easy these days. You'll have to put some water in your wine if you want to get along. You'll need to be delicate when it comes to handling certain issues. Don't try to solve everything at once; dealing with one thing at a time will be less stressful.

February

Your patience will have its limits and you'll feel on the verge of exploding on several occasions. You'll have a short fuse, and you may come into conflict with people quite easily. It would be best to avoid debating certain issues; you won't be flexible about your ideas. If you take some time for yourself and recharge your batteries, you'll be able to get along with others later.

HEALTH
You may experience periods of anxiety that will affect your mood and actions. Stress will result in stomach and digestion issues. It's best to watch your diet to make it easier for you to digest your food. Try to enjoy yourself and take care of yourself. This will be essential if you want to feel better.

WORK AND MONEY
It will be difficult to get to work in the morning. You'll have trouble sleeping, so you'll have trouble getting up. Working from home and having a flexible schedule could help you. Don't hesitate to talk to your boss. They will be a good listener. You may have plans to start a business, but the timing may not be right. It would be better to wait a little.

LOVE • SINGLES
Despite some attempts, it will be difficult for you to meet interesting people because your heart will not be in it. A few outings with friends will do you good and you'll be able to confide in them about your moods.

LOVE • COUPLES
You'll want to be tender, but your awkwardness could scare your partner away. You'll need to find the right words to express your feelings. If you experience daily conflicts in your relationship, it could be difficult to restore your intimacy afterwards. Instead, try to control your impulsiveness and be gentle.

March

The arrival of spring will have a great effect on you and will make your winter blues go away. You'll have a new project that will occupy your free time. You'll enjoy good times with your family and your *joie de vivre* could be reborn. You'll be on a roll! You'll make your loved ones happy.

HEALTH
Your mental health will be in a precarious place, but you'll use some tools to avoid falling back into negative patterns. You could use the help of a therapist. This will help you set helpful goals for yourself. By taking charge of your life, you will have everything you need to finally be happy.

WORK AND MONEY
The atmosphere at work will be pleasant and enjoyable. You'll find new motivation to invest yourself fully in your job and to work as a team. This could lead to a new collaboration with a partner that could bring you great rewards, in both personal and financial terms. Seize all opportunities!

LOVE • SINGLES
You'll meet some interesting people, but none of the relationships you form will be serious enough to tell your friends about. You'll have good times with no strings attached. This will change your mind and will make sure that you won't be alone some nights.

LOVE • COUPLES
You'll need to lay your cards on the table with your significant other to determine everyone's tasks in the house. Responsibilities must inevitably be shared to balance what needs to be done in the household. Starting a dialogue makes everything better. You will achieve a new harmony and your love will stay strong.

April

You'll want to get away from it all, whether it's through a move or a trip. You'll need a change of scenery. Great projects are on the horizon! You'll try an activity with family or friends that is out of your comfort zone and that will lead you to a new passion.

HEALTH

A drastic change in your diet will do you a world of good. You'll increase your energy and improve your overall well-being. "Tell me what you eat, and I will tell you who you are." This will be your new motto.

WORK AND MONEY

A change at work will be favorable and well received. You'll enjoy dealing with clients and you'll take advantage of new contacts to expand your network. You'll know how to plan to perform better later. You'll have lots of ideas!

LOVE • SINGLES

You'll want to be more active on social media—so much so that it may become difficult to manage. Try not to spread yourself too thin and stay focused on your primary goals. You don't need to chat with people that don't fit your criteria; you'll have to make some choices.

LOVE • COUPLES

You'll be happy to see peace return to your relationship! You'll experience a renewed passion. The chemistry between you and your partner will be back. Expect to share some sweet moments. Although the years pass, your love endures, and your bond stays strong.

May

You'll want to put your creativity to use by working on an artistic project that you've been thinking about for a while. Whether it's writing a book, a play, a movie, or a song, you'll be expressing what's inside you that you want to get out. You'll need to weigh the pros and cons of certain aspects of your life. Trust your judgment.

HEALTH
You will feel good in your body and mind because of some liberating revelations. You'll know how to handle stress and you'll be much calmer than you have been during the past few months. If you have skin problems, they will disappear like magic. Your body is sending you messages.

WORK AND MONEY
You don't need to make your decisions quickly. You'll have the time you need to do so. If you have important documents to sign, step back and consult a colleague if necessary. Spoken words fly away, but written words remain. Make sure the two are consistent, as you don't want to be fooled.

LOVE • SINGLES
Confiding in someone could lead to love! Someone you've known for a long time will confide in you and you'll know how to comfort them—so much so that you will end up in bed together. By talking openly about your sexuality, you will ignite something. Whether it's a flash in the pan or a lasting relationship, only time will tell …

LOVE • COUPLES
You'll want to break the routine and try new things in the bedroom. Your significant other will be more reluctant at first but will eventually follow your lead. Together, you will explore new horizons. Hours of passion and pleasure await you!

11

June

Your overactive imagination may play tricks on you. You may be imagining things that aren't actually real. Check your information carefully before blaming anyone else, as you could be the one responsible. A move will turn your life upside down. It could be a child leaving the family nest or a relative moving in with you.

HEALTH

You'll want to move more. You may take up running and cycling. Inevitably, you will increase your cardiovascular endurance and be in better physical shape. Sports will have a direct impact on your mental health as well.

WORK AND MONEY

Changes will have to be made at work and you'll decide to take the lead. With the help of your colleagues, you'll meet with management and get things done. There will be no stopping you; you will go all the way with your ideas.

LOVE • SINGLES

Although your fantasies do not coincide with reality, you'll spend hours dreaming about The One. However, it will be difficult to find a person on social media who meets all your criteria. It would be better to meet people in person to give them a chance. You might be surprised!

LOVE • COUPLES

You'll want to prove your love—with words, of course, but also with significant actions, such as buying your partner jewelry to symbolize your love. It doesn't matter what it is. It will make your significant other happy and that will make you happy.

July

Summer vacation is finally here! You'll be happy to break your routine and have fun doing all sorts of activities. You could go on an adventure with your family without planning an itinerary. Whether you're camping, staying at a hotel, or hanging out with friends, it doesn't matter; you'll have a lot of fun!

HEALTH
You will need to be careful with your carbohydrate intake. If you are over-weight, you could be at a higher risk for diabetes. Your alcohol intake will also need to be monitored. Remember: Moderation is key!

WORK AND MONEY
Luck may be on your side. A small lottery ticket could pay off big. Those who invest in the stock market could cash in with a nice surplus. This is a good time to save your money. As the saying goes, a penny saved is a penny earned. It's never too late to get started!

LOVE • SINGLES
A get-together with someone from another country could make your heart skip a beat. You'll have deep and sincere discussions. Distance may be an issue eventually, but for now, you'll have a good time together.

LOVE • COUPLES
You will experience magical moments with your significant other and you won't want them to end. You are in a beautiful period of your relationship and your love is stronger than ever. It has taken you a while to let go, but now that you have, you trust your partner and feel good.

August

A sense of lightness will come over you. You'll want to really let go during this period. Although this will do you a lot of good, you may not meet others' expectations, and this could create conflict. While it's good to let go and relax, you shouldn't be too nonchalant.

HEALTH
Routine tests may be ordered by your doctor and may reveal an issue. It won't be anything major if you follow the doctor's recommendations. The stress of the situation will still overwhelm you and it won't help your case.

WORK AND MONEY
You'll be successful at work and you'll receive congratulations from someone you care about. You will be touched by the attention you receive. This will give you the energy you need to keep working hard. You'll have the wind in your sails!

LOVE • SINGLES
While you will experience a beautiful and intense connection with someone, it could end suddenly for reasons beyond your control. Although this will affect you, you'll quickly move on. You'll decide to take a break from social media and focus on your friendships rather than your romantic relationships.

LOVE • COUPLES
You'll enjoy doing things with your partner; your bond will be palpable. You'll be inseparable and you'll want to enjoy your time together as much as possible. This will be a harmonious and peaceful period.

September

Everyone makes their own happiness. If you want to be happy, it must come from within. You'll experience emotional ups and downs, and you will question the very foundation of your beliefs. A spiritual quest could follow. Someone close to you will make revelations that will make you feel uneasy. You'll have to keep things in perspective to avoid worrying too much.

HEALTH
You may need to take a few days off work to recover from discomfort. It shouldn't last if you take care of things right away. You'll need to pay attention to your health, as there are a few ailments that may affect you. Diet and physical activity are key to feeling better.

WORK AND MONEY
You could use a little solitude to get on with your work, but it won't seem possible. You'll have to put out fires, which will delay the completion of your work projects. You will have to work overtime or bring work home to get everything done.

LOVE • SINGLES
Friendship will take precedence over your other relationships. You'll want to enjoy your moments of freedom and live life to the fullest without compromise. You'll be perfectly comfortable with your single life and this will work well for you for the time being.

LOVE • COUPLES
You'll need time for yourself. You'll be looking for a more active social life. Although your partner is your best ally, you'll need to surround yourself with others as well. Love is not exclusive for you, and you may want to look elsewhere. Think twice before you take the leap …

Scorpio

October

You'll be nostalgic for the summer that has just ended and sad about the colder weather that is slowly settling in. You'll need to keep yourself busy if you don't want to fall into a depression. Meditation and a new perspective could help you focus on what is essential. A few outings with family or friends will take your mind off things.

HEALTH
You'll need to take care of your mental health; it will all come down to good lifestyle habits. Any type of excess should be avoided, as you could easily develop addictive behaviors. The help of a therapist could be beneficial.

WORK AND MONEY
Calculate before you spend and avoid unnecessary purchases. You have savings but if you overspend, it could go down the drain quickly. You'll be offered a partnership at work that could be tempting. Pay attention to the terms of a contract to avoid surprises.

LOVE • SINGLES
It's easy to lie when no one can verify what you're saying! You'll meet someone who will seem very interesting at first, but who could be hiding a questionable past. Beware of smooth talkers and don't trust too easily. If something seems too good to be true, it probably is.

LOVE • COUPLES
You'll have difficulty understanding your significant other and meeting their demands. You'll have to be an excellent listener if you want to overcome the misunderstandings that invade your daily life. The moment of truth approaches; you'll have to reveal certain things if you want to evolve with your partner.

November

You will dream of traveling and getting away from it all. You'll do whatever it takes to break your routine. You'll take care of yourself, treating yourself to a skin treatment or a massage. You'll take the opportunity to catch up on your annual appointments and buy some new clothes. The month will go by so fast that you'll forget all about the gloomy weather!

HEALTH
Your blood pressure will be low, and you may have a few headaches. A little relaxation will help you get back on track. Your skin may be dry, so you'll need to stay hydrated, especially at this time of year. Drinking lots of water will make you feel better and will benefit your whole body.

WORK AND MONEY
You'll be busy at work and will find it hard to keep up. If you work in health care, you'll be so overwhelmed that you'll hardly be able to breathe. Luckily, you know how to handle this stress and won't bring it home. If you're thinking of retiring soon, plan your exit well to avoid leaving too much work behind.

LOVE • SINGLES
An ex will resurface, and this could upset your peace of mind. You'll take the opportunity to make some adjustments to make peace with the relationship once and for all. Although there are possible romantic partners lurking around, it will be difficult to get you out of your bubble. You're not in a hurry, and that's fine!

LOVE • COUPLES
You'll want to spend time daydreaming, but it will be hard to do so if you're not alone. A little change in the bedroom might inspire you and make you want to get closer to your significant other.

December

You'll feel the excitement of the holiday season, and you will want to make others happy. You'll spread your joy to others, whether it's through good food, volunteer work, or gift giving. It will also be time for you to make peace with someone you've been at odds with for a few months. You miss and care about them, so take the first steps toward reconciliation.

HEALTH

You may catch a virus that could linger for a few weeks if you don't do anything about it. Washing your hands regularly and distancing yourself from others will prevent you from spreading the virus to others, but it won't stop you from having a great holiday season!

WORK AND MONEY

You'll have to work even harder if you want to finish everything before the holidays. Don't hesitate to ask your colleagues for help. Everything is easier when you work together. There will be expenses at this time of year. Make sure you can afford to buy everything you have planned.

LOVE • SINGLES

A declaration of love out of the blue may surprise and delight you. This person could be a family friend or a long-time acquaintance. For the first time in a long time, you might be thinking about letting your guard down in a relationship. Will this be the end of your single life? You'll find out next year!

LOVE • COUPLES

You'll have a lot of fun organizing receptions with your significant other. Your powerful bond will make you realize that you are made for each other. Your strong chemistry and the beautiful moments you share will fill you with happiness.

Personality

Intense and spirited

Scorpio natives are strong, powerful, determined, and proud in everything they do. They're intense and passionate, mainly in terms of sexuality. They start every new life adventure with enthusiasm. They know exactly what they want and will always finish what they start. Some may call them excessive, not only in their leisure time, but also in their work.

Scorpios face every day with sensitivity and intelligence. Nothing is left to chance. They can be ruthless and dominating; however, they also have an iron will that allows them to get astonishing results.

Scorpios are often brilliant and they use their smarts to their advantage. That's why they're so involved in everything they do. This aspect of their personality can explain why some Scorpios are purists and perfectionists. When they get involved in a cause, they don't do it halfway!

Scorpio natives have strong characters and tend to be jealous. This doesn't only apply to love. Watch out if you get a position or prize that they believe should have been theirs. You may become the object of their cruel torment and scathing comments. You might as well be warned and be sympathetic towards them.

These natives are very ambitious and rarely confide in others. They're secretive and prefer keeping their emotions or aspirations to themselves. This can explain why they tend to be jealous and vengeful. By refusing to reveal their inner selves, they leave room for assumptions that might not be true.

Scorpios are industrious workers. As soon as they've clearly set their goals, they throw their body and mind into their projects knowing exactly what to do and how. Thankfully, they pursue most of their projects with good intentions. Many Scorpios are among the world's greatest visionaries. They can become great builders. However, just as they can build, so can they destroy.

When they make decisions, they need to have a freedom of choice; otherwise, they can rebel. Scorpios are proud and generous. That's why they can aspire to the top positions and succeed in their projects, as long as they put their whole heart and intelligence in them. Scorpio natives can be insecure, but they aren't less intelligent than other people. However, they can be meaner and more selfish.

With their temperament, Scorpios make great, albeit strict, leaders. They usually become authoritarian bosses who demand that their employees comply with the rules and be disciplined. They don't take well to mistakes and demand obedience.

Scorpios are energetic. When they know how to use their energy efficiently, they have great endurance. They will never give up when faced with failure. They'll continue to fight for victory, ignoring obstacles and crushing anyone who

gets in the way of their success. The Scorpio sign was
once symbolized by the
eagle, showing the natives'
rigidity, but also illustrating
their ability to overcome obstacles.

No one remains indifferent to
the Scorpios they meet. We
know at first glance whether
we'll like them. There aren't
any gray areas, and Scorpios
think the same way.

Scorpios make their own
luck, through personal efforts
and perseverance. They usually don't rely on anyone but
themselves to achieve their
goals.

Being very intense, they usually don't accept inactivity and monotony. They're
not afraid of change; in fact, they welcome it. They have no problem progress-
ing from one life stage to another. In fact, they can cause chaos just because
they want to experience something new and interesting.

Independent and assertive

Sexuality plays a predominant role in Scorpios' lives. For those who aren't natives of this sign, it can be hard to imagine just how far they'll go in their erotic
pursuits. They don't hold back at all. They don't repress or ignore their powerful instincts. They usually give in to their impulses and aren't too concerned
with offending or hurting others with their attitude.

They have a developed ego and express themselves openly. They can be
aggressive and overcritical, making harsh comments and inappropriate jokes.
They can even take perverse pleasure in acting this way.

Scorpio natives are very assertive. That's why they tend to be successful when they're well adjusted. They're intellectual and sensitive, and they have strong willpower. They have what it takes to reach their full potential.

Scorpios act independently. They don't need the approval or opinion of others to make decisions; however, this doesn't mean that they constantly disagree with others or never follow the rules. They're very much aware of their responsibilities. They still give themselves the right to evaluate and choose their own code of conduct.

If Scorpio's ruling planets, Mars and Pluto, are not well aligned, natives may repress their emotions and sexuality. Everything they repress will then be expressed subliminally. This can take the form of aggressive behavior and cruelty, among other things. Moreover, this can happen out of nowhere, without anyone seeing it coming.

Will and intelligence

Scorpio natives are very self-confident and don't really care about what other people think. They don't need outside approval because they believe they have the appropriate judgment to make their decisions and to adapt to different situations.

Unlike the other signs of the zodiac, Scorpios rarely use their sexuality negatively, such as through aggression or pettiness.

Male Scorpios are romantics at heart. When they're in love, they can be the most sensual and passionate partners. Jeal-

ousy, however, can threaten their relationship. Their love life must be satisfactory; otherwise, there will be trouble in paradise.

Scorpios are loyal friends and partners, and they demand the same thing from others. Nothing is taken lightly. They're ready to do anything to help a friend in need, but people have to know how to win their friendship.

Scorpios are ambitious and enjoy the good life. They'll do anything to accumulate as much material wealth as possible and purchase luxury items such as a nice house or fancy clothes. Being naturally generous, though, they share this wealth and spoil their loved ones.

They are driven, extreme, and rebellious, and this can cause a lot of pain around them. Pluto and Mars are responsible for this reputation as they largely influence Scorpios' character.

Scorpio natives can be jealous and possessive, and they have a lot of trouble managing these faults. They don't fear rejection and aren't prone to anxiety like some other signs; their problem lies in their self-image. When they love someone, they do so passionately and completely. The object of the Scorpio's affection becomes a part of them, so when they suffer a loss or abandonment, they feel as though they've been betrayed. It's as if their entire self had been attacked.

Scorpios' boastful and secretive character can be explained by their tendency to be selfish and introverted. They don't care about the approval of others. Even under pressure, they always feel free to live according to their own judgment. They're powerful and always in perfect control of themselves.

Scorpio natives are positive and interested in humanitarian activities. They're concerned by societal problems and try their best to help those in need. Life's mysteries also interest them a lot; they like talking about philosophy, the occult, and paranormal phenomena.

Although Scorpios are self-confident, they still have their insecurities. When they're in groups, they seem more detached and less available, but when they have to face emotional problems alone, they struggle more than most of the other signs due to their numerous inner conflicts.

Scorpios are vindictive and proud, and they don't forgive and forget easily. They can hold a grudge for a long time if their expectations aren't met. They don't tolerate any kind of outrage, insults, or verbal abuse. They seek revenge immediately, but this never heals their damaged pride.

Scorpios are incredibly smart and keen. That's why it's always surprising to see them acting out of jealousy, possessiveness, or revenge. They can address these faults through controlling their emotions and reactions. That way, they'll have fewer enemies and won't waste as much mental energy.

Scorpios tend to work on these faults because they're smart enough to understand that it's the only way for them to fully grow as a person.

Excess and dominance

One negative aspect of Scorpios' personality is their desire to dominate. They love taking on leadership roles. When they do, they tend to demand a lot from their subordinates rather than ask appropriately. They impose blind obedience and have little tolerance for error. As a result, it can be hard for them to make friends, but they're always sure to get what they want!

Their intolerant and critical attitude towards others can compromise many of their projects. Thankfully, they're smart enough to notice it and attempt to remedy it.

The negative tendencies of Scorpio natives can sometimes be explained by their hypersexuality. They don't always take moral principles into account. Their behavior is their business and they're the only ones to decide what they do. Unfortunately, they don't seem to realize that indulging in their sexual excesses hurts others as well as themselves.

If they fall on the more extreme end of the spectrum, they'll be obsessed with sex, which can affect their mental health and sensitivity in all other aspects of life.

Of course, humans have different sexual needs. What can be tempting for one may be less attractive to another; however, to avoid problems, Scorpios should not let pushing boundaries become a way of life. Scorpio natives must be careful to keep their libido under control and not to abuse it.

Predispositions

Scorpio natives are studious, and they prefer practical research to abstract reasoning. They're not afraid of working hard and pursuing lengthy studies, namely in specialized medical fields such as surgery or psychiatry. They tend to dream of expressing their authority and subjecting others to their will. They often become soldiers or sailors, and these roles teach them the foundations of obedience.

Scorpios are often stubborn and inflexible; they do everything they can to achieve the goals they set for themselves. They have endless energy in their professional and personal lives, and have everything they need to become extremely successful. They are never satisfied with second place and always target the top spot. They work relentlessly and put in the time and effort needed to get the job done. Their energy allows them to recharge quickly and accomplish even the most arduous tasks. They are responsible and born to be leaders.

To dedicate themselves to their work, Scorpio natives must know why it matters. They're not interested in meaningless tasks. They especially like fields that require lots of problem solving. Being an investigator, for example, is perfect for them because they must solve a mystery, which they really enjoy. They can also be great psychologists or physicians as they must identify, analyze, and solve their patients' issues. Although they're willing to contribute to the well-being of others, Scorpios can also use their intelligence for sinister causes, designing their plans meticulously and discreetly. Scorpios like anything done privately and stealthily. When they don't get what they want, they get frustrated and take it out on those they envy.

Scorpios excel at careers in fields requiring precision, such as medicine, surgery, physics, and dentistry. They also stand out in other fields, such as finance, mechanics, engineering, manufacturing, sales, and politics.

Scorpios are intrigued by mysteries, so they perform especially well in cryptography and occultism. They like exploring people's souls and unveiling their secrets.

Scorpios consider their success to be guaranteed. It can't be any other way. Given their great potential and natural skills, many Scorpios will achieve their goals.

2, 3, 5, 7, 11, 13, 17, 19, 23, 29, 31, 37, 41, 43, 47, 53, 59, 61, 67, 71, 73, 79, 83, 89, 97.

Love

Faithful but vengeful

Scorpio natives tend to hide their emotions. They hide under their shell to protect their pride and to conceal their fragile and vulnerable side. Despite everything, as lovers, they throw themselves into passion and excess.

Scorpios have one essential value when it comes to love: faithfulness. They stay true to their partners and expect them to do the same. They tend to be jealous, so they sometimes have trouble trusting their partners. They're suspicious of them and will hound them with questions if they're the least bit doubtful.

If their partner is unfaithful, or if the relationship simply doesn't work out, Scorpios will feel abandoned and take it badly. Instead of feeling sorry for themselves, they'll get angry and want to exact revenge. It's not easy splitting up with a Scorpio!

Health

Sexual and misunderstood

Scorpios are usually linked to the most brutal human emotions. As a result, they are probably the most misunderstood of the zodiac signs. This is largely due to Scorpios' intense nature. They're seen as clever, vengeful, and hypersexual. Although their sign controls the sexual organs, not all Scorpios are hypersexual. Above all, they have strong physical needs, but not necessarily sexual ones. Their determination allows them lose interest in people quickly. They can be extremely passionate when they're in a relationship, which could explain why they come off as sexual beings.

Scorpios must avoid repressing their strongest sexual feelings. Because their sign controls the lymphatic system, they must quickly get rid of physical and emotional excesses. If not, they'll be more prone anger, severe back pains, or painful menstrual cramps.

Scorpios need to experience all feelings, good or bad. Their tendency to let negativity take over sometimes leads Scorpios to develop psychosomatic illnesses. Since they're very energetic, they luckily bounce back quickly.

Scorpios aren't moderate people; it's all or nothing. They'll eat, smoke, and drink excessively or won't do any of that at all. They're passionate about art, mechanics, and good food.

Original and unusual flavors

Scorpios are not natural gourmets, but they like trying new things and enjoy unique or unusual dishes, which they'll have for the rest of their life if they enjoy them. They especially like exotic and original foods and avoid dry options such as nuts.

Characteristics

Who's always ready to fight back?
Who prefers to act anonymously?
Who's a fervent friend or a subtle enemy?
Scorpio!

The Sign of the Builder

Symbol: Scorpion

Element: Water

Quality: Set

Ruling Planet: Pluto

Color: Red

Metal: Steel

Stone: Garnet

Perfume: Sandalwood

Keywords: Intense, penetrating, secretive

House: Eight (procreation, life, death, rebirth, sexuality, mysteries, occultism)

Mythology

The Scorpio constellation immortalizes the giant scorpion sent by the goddess Artemis to kill Orion, a renowned hunter who tried to kill every creature on Earth. After Orion's death, he and the Scorpion were transformed into constellations.

Qualities and Faults

Qualities: Passionate, powerful, emotional, committed, loyal, imaginative, thoughtful, subtle, perseverant, determined

Faults: Jealous, resentful, stubborn, merciless, inflexible, secretive, suspicious, vindictive

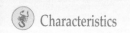

The Scorpio Body

Governed body parts: Reproductive system, lymphatic system

Acupuncture meridian: Bladder

Diseases: Cystitis, genitourinary disorders, hemorrhoids, premenstrual syndrome

Foods: Prune, hops

Associations

Herbs and plants: Aloe, rose hip, broom, capers, cactus, garlic, ginger, ginseng, horseradish, lentil, radish, thistle

Objects: Chess, cars, novels, magnifying glasses, vault, tarot cards, ornaments

Professions and trades: Analyst, butcher, businessperson, chemist, detective, farmer, financial adviser, police officer, plumber, psychologist, researcher, soldier, surgeon, physician, public servant, entrepreneur, pharmacist

Sports and leisure: Fine dining, psychology, caving, scuba diving, puzzles, occultism

Scorpio and the World

The Scorpio symbolizes world resources, international finances, multinationals, and the death or rebirth of nations. It's closely linked to secret societies and the occult.

Friendship

Faithful and complex

Scorpios don't become friends with just anyone. To befriend a Scorpio, one must earn their trust while trying to avoid mistakes. The slightest error could lead to disaster. When Scorpios are sure that everything is mutual, they'll then grant their friendship.

Scorpios are discreet, loyal, and trustworthy friends. Friendships mean everything to them. As suspicious with their friends as they are with their lovers, they expect to get what they give all the time. The slightest misunderstanding or mistake will set them off.

Being a Scorpio's friend can be challenging. They're complex and don't like simple things and relationships. They can even be insulted by something that was meant to be a compliment! If they're not stubborn, they'll get along with other water signs. They're also rarely attracted to air signs; however, they get along with Virgos, as long as they can accept their criticism.

Faults and Weaknesses

Withdrawn and scared of rejection

Scorpios are real enigmas. They seldom show their feelings, desires, and motivations. They develop this emotional shell early on, which only hardens with age. This reflects their fear of being hurt, which they won't admit to anyone; however, it quickly becomes second nature and an enormous flaw.

They hide their feelings so well that they sometimes manage to forget who they are. Before figuring that out, though, they'll often reach the point of no return. They can make themselves sick trying to sort things out.

Manipulative and pushy

In searching for the truth, Scorpios don't always use the most efficient methods. Their way of doing things is usually very painful for them and their loved ones.

They'll often try to obtain answers forcefully or using manipulation. For example, they'll assess their loved ones' loyalty by pushing them away, lying to them, and testing their honesty. By pushing their loved ones' personal limits to see when they'll crack, they bring people to their wit's end. In love, they'll pretend to be someone they're not with their partner to prove to themselves that they still have charm.

What's ironic is that Scorpios refuse to take part in any pettiness. They hate hypocrisy, lies, and manipulation. Their actions are spontaneous and depend on which side of the bed they woke up that morning. The Taurus, their opposite sign, usually chooses a more relaxed and indulgent approach. Scorpios are too tortured inwardly to see through their emotions clearly, and they then become their worst enemy. If they took their Taurus buddies as examples, they'd learn how to cool down once in a while!

Work

Scorpios' vigorousness and aggressiveness lead them to spend all their energy on their work. They're passionate people; they invest fully in various projects and expect the same from others. The results must measure up to the efforts they put in, and they set the bar high! They're serious in everything they undertake and are tenacious. Their work must allow them to take on ambitious challenges to satisfy their desire for power. They work hard and boast exceptional concentration. Work doesn't scare them!

Explosive and strong-willed

Scorpios are strong-willed, and their dedication to their work is sincere. They're bright, determined, and controlling. They constantly encounter roadblocks, however, because of their eternal desire to succeed. It's not surprising, as they tend to suffer with internal conflict. For them, it's all or nothing! They should let go sometimes, but they're always ready to fight to the very end. They can then  have explosive emotions. If they're bosses, they dedicate themselves entirely to work and push limits to the extreme. Scorpio employees are clever and conscientious, as long as they respect their colleagues. However, only Scorpios know their own true intentions.

Home

Comfortable and neat

As with all water signs, Scorpios are usually very attached to their home. This strong feeling isn't necessarily visible at first, but it's there. They like caring for their home themselves so that it can be exactly to their liking. They reject the ideas of others because they know what they want. They opt for a beautifully decorated home that is welcoming and neat. However, they don't care about appearances and prefer comfort to beauty.

When it comes to home life, there are two Scorpio personality types. The first type prefers a warm home, and when they decide to stay in a specific area, they do whatever they can to make it comfortable for everyone. The second type is eternally tormented. They like their living space but try to suppress their desire to stay home. Without really knowing why, they fight their own instincts and refuse to stay home, even if they're comfortable there.

Emotional and in search of a permanent home

For Scorpios, the home is a primarily emotional place. They don't choose decor because they think it will be admired. They must feel emotionally connected to their living space. They make choices according to their feelings and their home usually reflects this.

Although many Scorpios move regularly and ostensibly without any emotion, these changes make them feel very anxious. They will maintain a facade but, deep inside, they sting themselves. As soon as they feel like they're in the right place, though, they'll be ready to follow their instincts and live there forever.

Success

Strategic and power-hungry

Scorpios are power-hungry, ready to do whatever it takes to move up the ladder and get what they want. Their success isn't measured by their bank account, but rather by the control they have over themselves and the people close to them. They strategize to destabilize their opponents and ensure victory. Even when they win, people can't figure out their thoughts or feelings. They're so discreet that they're a mystery to most people. Be that as it may, they always express their satisfaction through their comments, behavior, and personal style.

Only their close friends and lovers will get to enjoy their generosity following their achievements. They don't share their happiness or assets with others as they're always on the lookout for potential enemies.

Scorpios who hold positions of authority aren't known to be friendly; they're rarely selfless. They often boldly try to take advantage of new opportunities or embark upon adventures that others don't dare to undertake. They usually try to turn situations to their advantage.

Rivalry

Competitive and combative

Scorpios are naturally determined and intense, and make formidable adversaries. They're familiar with power struggles and will stop at nothing to win.

They always want to reach the top and love competition. They're not motivated by the spoils of victory; all they want is to be number one!

Bold and energetic

Scorpios are seldom discouraged. As soon as they're faced with obstacles, they dive in headfirst. Instead of thinking things through, they're stimulated and galvanized by the challenge. They need this stimulation and energy to thrive. They go all in when they need to confront people or situations.

Discreet and guarded

Scorpios aim for the top in all spheres of life. The advantage they have over their opponents is that they rarely talk about their goals. Others may think they lack interest and let their guards down in response, but they are no match for the Scorpio!

Social Life

Popular but selective

Scorpio natives are charming friends and lovers. Despite their popularity, they're discreet and serious, and will act demurely during dinners and outings with friends.

They're incredibly loyal to and protective of their loved ones. They'll be part of several diverse groups. They prefer people who aren't the most popular; they don't care about popularity and will reach out to people regardless of social status. The only downside to their friendship is that they tend to be more possessive than protective, and can become jealous easily.

Scorpios almost always exercise safe and discerning judgment. Their intelligence almost allows them to read people's thoughts, which makes them very hard to fool and hide information from. Still, they're naturally suspicious people and their prejudices make them act irrationally. By shedding these false impressions, they'll learn to better accept things as they really are.

Confident and independent

Scorpios have great confidence in their own abilities. They choose and organize their social and leisure activities themselves. They tend to dislike organized social activities. As a result, you'll never see them going on organized trips or to crowded places for social events. They don't need anyone planning their downtime. After all, who knows them better than themselves?

Appearance

Superior and uncompromising

Scorpios tend to have wide faces with prominent foreheads. Their flat cheek-bones contrast well with their full lips. They have droopy lids over piercing eyes. They're either sturdy without being too muscular or small and agile.

Scorpio natives are hard to read. They don't tend to confide much and prefer being mysterious. Their gaze is so evocative, though, that it usually betrays them; you can read their emotions if you stare at them long enough.

Despite their reluctance to reveal their emotions, Scorpios' eyes can reveal their hidden feelings. When they're moved, their nostrils even tend to twitch!

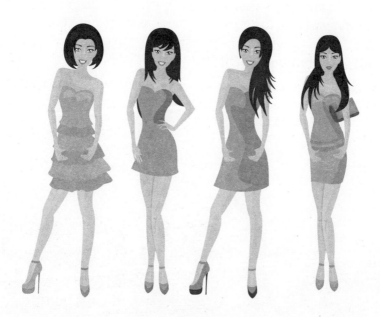

Sexuality

Passionate and ardent

Scorpios are sexually open. They're passionate beings and will either love you or hate you. They're enthusiastic lovers and never cease to amaze and surprise their partners.

Despite being fantastic lovers, Scorpios can unfortunately ruin their relationships if they give in to jealousy or possessiveness. Scorpios aren't selfish lovers, however, and enjoy pleasing their partners. They see sexuality as an opportunity to deepen the emotional mysteries of the human soul. Through their sexuality, Scorpios reveal an obscure side of their personality that they often repress outside of relationships.

Scorpios are probably incompatible with reserved and shy people because they might be too intense and passionate for them. Pair a Scorpio with an extrovert, however, and sparks will definitely fly!

Scorpio Affinities in the Zodiac

With an Aries
(from March 21 to April 20)

Can the stubborn Aries and the possessive Scorpio get along? It's possible! They both have vivacious and uncompromising personalities. We can't really see them getting together if all they do is contradict one another. This tournament of words and gestures would tire anyone else out, but they seem to find renewed energy in it.

With a Taurus

(from April 21 to May 20)

The solid, placid, and balanced Taurus is grounded and is a sign of great material success. Their balance makes up for the Scorpio's deficiencies. Together, they can climb social and professional ladders very easily.

With a Gemini

(from May 21 to June 21)

This pairing is often unhealthy because there isn't enough balance between the partners. The Scorpio is so authoritarian that they need someone who can hold their own. It's not that Geminis lack personality (theirs are dual!), but they're divided against themselves, and can even be hesitant. The Scorpio doesn't hesitate to dominate, and their conflicts can become too much to bear.

With a Cancer
(from June 22 to July 22)

This pairing is often successful. The sentimental and family-oriented Cancer prefers to get along with others rather than to fight, while the sensitive Scorpio is ready to make compromises as long as they don't have negative consequences.

With a Leo
(from July 23 to August 23)

This pairing consists of two strong personalities. Neither will want to give in, but they do enjoy each other a lot, mostly because of their appreciation of all things sensual. The Scorpio does risk getting bored and may want to stray, but the Leo catches up to them. They may fight and reconcile. This couple has their issues, but they can make it work.

With a Virgo

(from August 24 to September 22)

These signs are very different. Scorpios are libertarian and libertine, while Virgos are more domesticated.

Scorpios may complain about home life, but they'll find this cozy and serene existence charming as long as their Virgo partner listens to and caters to them.

With a Libra

(from September 23 to October 23)

Opposites attract, but not in this case. The quarrelsome and spiteful Scorpio doesn't usually get along with the more refined Libra. Often, according to the laws of contrasts, the diplomatic Libra can be a source of comfort for the Scorpio, but the irritable Scorpio sometimes finds this annoying given their appetite for destruction.

With a Scorpio
(from October 24 to November 22)

Two Scorpios are so much alike, that this can be a blessing or a curse. They fight, compromise, and make up just as easily.

With a Sagittarius
(from November 23 to December 21)

These two fighters are equally ambitious, social, and sensual, and thus this pairing can be very successful. There will be clashes, but they reconcile quickly.

With a Capricorn

(from December 22 to January 20)

Theoretically, this pairing shouldn't work out, since the signs are so different—but it often does! The Capricorn's practicality and meticulousness make up for the Scorpio's irrationality. The Capricorn will manage the budget that the Scorpio often neglects. They understand that agreeing is better than fighting.

With an Aquarius

(from January 21 to February 19)

Scorpios and Aquarians share interest in the metaphysical, the occult, and philosophy. This pairing is a bit too superficial to sustain a household, and may not last.

47

With a Pisces
(from February 20 to March 20)

The Scorpio often dominates the Pisces. The Pisces is always a little elusive and escapes if they feel overly dominated. A more nuanced compromise can actually be established, and the two can influence one other. The only thing is that the Scorpio always needs to feel like they're in charge because they hate any kind of opposition or complaint.

Astro-baby

Characteristics

Scorpio babies are full of energy and have a piercing gaze. They have irresistible charm and quickly show their leadership skills. While at times hard to follow, they are determined and tenacious. Scorpio babies are seemingly independent and insensitive to strangers, but they treat their loved ones with love and affection.

Parents' advice

Scorpio children can channel their competitiveness and boisterous energy into sports or martial arts. They are intuitive and insightful, and they must understand that sometimes they must give in and be more trusting. They tend to hold grudges and don't forget when they get hurt or embarrassed. Parents must teach them forgiveness and help them to express their hidden emotions and feelings.

1st decan from October 24 to November 2

Little Scorpios' ambition and determination will be obvious from the start. As soon as they learn to walk, they assert themselves as exceptional leaders and organizers. They also know how to make friends easily, but their bossiness can cause issues. Show them all the advantages of being sensitive and kind towards their friends. They'll really need it!

2nd decan from November 3 to 12

These Scorpio babies display great creativity and the ability to express their emotions and feelings warmly. They want to see the world! They go on adventures, enjoying each experience they encounter along the way. Moreover, it's during one of their many adventures that they'll learn the advantages of perseverance and hard work.

3rd decan from November 13 to 22

These bubbly babies live life so intensely that you'll sometimes have a hard time following them. These Scorpio babies are more extroverted than the two other decans; they'll be sociable and passionate in everything they do. They'll truly be fun to watch!

When Scorpios have something in mind, nothing can stop them. They'll reach their goals with such determination that they'll make it look easy.